baby massage

baby massage

expert know-how at your fingertips

Gayle Berry

illustrations by Bo Lundberg

MQP

introduction   **6**

the gift of touch   **8**

getting started   **28**

head-to-toe massage   **46**

massage & movement   **78**

index   **94**

introduction

Massage is a wonderful and special pleasure that you can share with your baby.
Baby massage is not new. This ancient art has been used in diverse cultures
across the world for thousands of years to boost physical and mental development,
encourage emotional bonding, and promote relaxation.

Babies crave skin contact. Touch is your baby's most developed
sense at birth, and through it you can communicate with baby
immediately. Everyone has the ability to touch and massage. You do
not need any qualifications to massage your baby. Massage is
simply a technique that helps reinforce the natural power of touch.

Baby massage has well-established benefits for you and your
child. Integrating massage into your relationship gives you another
way to get to know and understand each other. Massage eases
your baby's transition from the womb into the world and can help
stimulate development. Above all, it enables you both to relax and
have fun together.

Massage offers you the opportunity to communicate love, comfort,
and support to your baby. It allows you to interpret subtle nonverbal
language and develops your ability to listen. When you massage
your baby you lay down foundations of trust and security that will
help you build a happy and confident relationship for the future.

All babies—boys and girls—love massage. The skin contact and the close communication involved in this most relaxing exercise will delight your baby.
NB: Two chapters refer to girls and two to boys in order to avoid constant repetition of "he" or "she" in the text. Remember, the procedures described apply to all babies.

1   the gift of touch

a timeless art

The word "massage" derives from an Arabic word meaning "to stroke." There are historical accounts of massage being used in ancient civilizations as far back as 3000 years ago. There are even visual records—cave paintings have been discovered illustrating early forms of massage.

Although many Eastern cultures have recognized the benefits of massage for thousands of years—the art is practiced widely in China, India, Thailand, Indonesia, and Japan—massage was only introduced to Europe as a method of treating physical ailments in the nineteenth century by Swedish physiotherapist Henrik Ling. Today, massage is used by many people—from athletes to cancer patients—to enhance physical wellbeing, promote relaxation, and support the efficiency of many body systems.

It is difficult to say where the practice of baby massage originated. Certainly it has been widely used in India for hundreds of years—the art is passed down from mother to daughter. Baby massage became popular in the West during the 1970s after observers in India reported its therapeutic benefits. It was noted that babies in India, even in often poor material circumstances, seemed to thrive and be content despite their "deprivation." Some attributed this to a daily massage.

Babies in India have been enjoying the benefits of massage for hundreds of years. Baby massage is now widely practiced in the Western world.

Baby massage is now routinely used in hospitals in the United Kingdom and North America to support premature babies, and baby massage classes for new parents can be found in many areas.

why massage your baby?

Infant massage is beneficial for you and your baby in so many ways. Studies show that touch not only aids your growing baby's development, but also helps you grow in confidence as a parent, and develop an understanding of this new, special person in your life. The main benefits are summarized below.

relieves discomfort

During the first few months of life, your baby may suffer from a number of minor but uncomfortable complaints. One of the most common of these is gas. Doctors believe that babies swallow air while feeding. Their immature digestive systems can't expel it, so it becomes trapped. A distressing form of gas, known as colic, is symptomized by prolonged bouts of crying; pain when passing gas; a hard, tense stomach; and bringing the knees to the chest in discomfort. Relief from colic and gas is an important benefit of baby massage. Massage can tone the digestive tract, expel gas from the body, and break down large air bubbles, making them easier for your baby to pass. Massage may also help ease constipation—this is particularly useful when your baby starts eating solid food.

Massaging around the mouth and gums can bring relief from the pain of teething; over the sinuses, it eases congestion by helping drain mucus from the nasal passages.

Massage is a great way to ease the various the discomforts babies often suffer in their first few months. Soothing hands work wonders for the pains of colic and teething.

soothes baby's skin

Applying oils to your baby's skin can help improve its overall condition. This is particularly useful if your baby suffers from dry skin, eczema, or cradle cap.

Skin stimulation and touch allow a mother and child to bond, and create a calming and soothing atmosphere with plenty of all-important eye contact.

heightens skin contact

Skin is the first organ your baby develops in the womb and it is made of the same embryonic tissue as the brain. The skin is as thirsty for sensory experience as the brain. The effects of skin contact, and the lack of it, are profound.

The importance of touch for babies is now well known, but this has not always been the case. In the early nineteenth century, there was a high death rate in babies under the age of one who were raised in orphanages. This caused concern, especially as the babies were being provided with food, warmth, and shelter. What these infants lacked was skin contact or touch from their caregivers; they were handled only when absolutely necessary. This lack of touch and skin stimulation hampered the development of the babies' body systems. The infants became depressed, withdrawn, and eventually died. They were said to suffer from "marasmus," a Greek term meaning "wasting away."

encourages stimulating touch

As humans, we behave very differently toward our young than many other mammals. Dogs and cats lick their litters all over after birth. This is not just to clean them, but to stimulate the body systems to start working efficiently. Stimulation of the skin also helps the mother bond with her young by allowing her to impart her smell, helping each to recognize the other. This is vital in the process of a mother accepting her young, so it is essential to the survival of the young animals. We do not behave in this way with our babies, but simple actions such as making contact skin to skin, talking to your baby, and establishing eye contact are important in creating and encouraging bonds.

creates lasting bonds

Bonding with your baby is a complex process that develops over time through understanding and communication. It does not always happen immediately and there is no set time in which you must bond; the opportunity is never lost. Bonding is very important between parent and baby: it not only ensures the survival of the infant, it safeguards the emotional state of the parent.

Your baby needs you to feel a bond with her so her needs are met and she is protected and nurtured. Bonding is as important for a mother's emotional and mental health after birth—one factor involved in postnatal depression in new mothers could be the feeling that they have not bonded with their baby. Massage encourages bonding by creating the perfect environment for touch, eye contact, exchange of personal odors, and vocalizing (singing and talking) between mother and baby—all important aspects of the bonding process.

makes you relaxed together

Massage has powerful two-way benefits for babies and parents. Apart from its obvious usefulness in helping with specific conditions such as teething, colic, and constipation, it's an excellent way to aid relaxation and reduce stress and tension for both you and your baby. Regular massage sessions make your baby feel wonderfully relaxed— and she knows that this sensation is coming directly from you. Consequently, she learns to associate these good feelings of wellbeing with massage, and will look forward to her sessions.

did you know?

We are all born with the capacity to bond

- you are biologically designed to bond with your baby after birth through the release of prolactin and oxytocin, the "feel-good" hormones that encourage feelings of love and nurturing toward your baby.
- eye contact is very important in encouraging bonds between mother and baby. Studies show that your baby is attracted to the shape of your iris and pupil, and will become excited and responsive when exposed to this shape.
- singing and talking to your baby helps you bond with her. Research reveals that a mother is able to distinguish her baby's cry from others as early as three days after birth.
- even if you don't think you are aware of your baby's smell at birth, studies demonstrate that after just two hours of exposure to their newborns, 80 percent of mothers could distinguish their baby's clothes from those of other babies by smell alone.

the balance of hormones

Without the "stress reaction" hormone cortisol, we would not be able to react quickly enough to avoid potential harm. However, when its level becomes too high, we begin to experience negative effects. Symptoms include loss of appetite, insomnia, muscle cramps, headaches, and sweats.

When we encounter danger or feel threatened, the body produces hormones called cortisols that help us respond to a situation quickly by raising blood pressure, increasing heart rate, and preparing muscles for movement. These hormones are important in helping us react effectively in a threatening situation, so they are essential for survival. But they can also stay in the body and cause problems.

When skin is massaged, the body produces the hormones prolactin and oxytocin. These help lower levels of stress hormones in the body and help combat symptoms of stress. They are very valuable in the body after childbirth for mother and baby. Prolactin is responsible for the production of milk in the mother's breasts, and oxytocin has been linked to the promotion of mothers' nurturing feelings toward their babies.

Prolactin and oxytocin are also important for the baby. Birth can be the biggest threat to a baby's survival. To prepare a baby's body for birth, it is flooded with cortisols to help her react to threats or danger. Sometimes after a baby is born, particularly following a difficult birth, levels of these hormones remain high in the bloodstream, causing her to suffer stress symptoms. Because it increases the production of prolactin and oxytocin in your baby's body, massage is a vital tool in lowering her levels of stress.

happy and thriving

If you have had a massage, you will be familiar with the sensation of wellbeing it evokes and the release of tension it brings throughout the body. Your baby, too, will experience these sensations when you massage her. A happy, relaxed baby is more likely to eat well, sleep well, and have a good temperament. A happy baby helps make happy parents! If your baby is feeling relaxed, you are more likely to feel relaxed, which is important in the early days of parenting when it can feel as if you are on a steep learning curve.

warm, loving touch

Always have clean, warm hands when massaging your baby. Also, make sure that your nails are not too long and do not have jagged, rough edges that might make her feel uncomfortable.

have fun together

The mood of a massage session has a key impact. Basically, it should be relaxed, playful, and happy. Having fun with your baby and exchanging smiles and laughing together during a massage are important in helping build a relationship of love and trust. Massage helps teach your baby about the importance of feeling relaxed and happy. Your baby learns about the world through your reactions and responses to it. If you feel relaxed around your baby and demonstrate this to her, she will respond by being happy and relaxed.

vital stimulation

Massage helps encourage your baby's development by providing her with the skin stimulation she craves and by boosting the circulation to muscles, making her stronger and more physically able. Her brain is stimulated by the new sensations and experiences. By evoking all your baby's senses through massage, you teach her about social behavior, language, and movement, helping her reach her developmental goals.

A daily massage also increases your baby's stimulation levels. By stimulating her nervous system, touch produces new connections between body and brain. The more developed a baby's nervous system, the better equipped she is to cope with stimulation such as bright lights, loud noises, and strange smells.

Massaging your baby stimulates her nervous system and boosts circulation to the muscles, making her stronger and more alert.

key benefits

In addition to the beneficial effect of massage on your baby's nervous system, it also helps to promote the health of her other major body systems.

muscle system Babies have developed muscles at birth and are actually very strong despite their size. As your baby puts on weight and becomes more active, her muscles start to strengthen, permitting greater physical achievements, including developmental goals such as rolling over, sitting up, crawling, and walking.

skeletal system Your baby has a fully formed skeleton at birth. You may have noticed gaps between the plates of her skull—most evident at the top of the head—called fontanelles. They may remain open for 12–24 months after birth. Fontanelles are the result of a very important design feature of your baby's skull. The plates of bone in the skull do not fuse in the womb, enabling your baby to travel safely along the birth canal without the skull or brain being damaged or crushed.

circulatory system While your baby is in the womb she shares your circulatory system via the umbilical cord and placenta. This shared circulatory system brings oxygen and nutrients to your baby and removes carbon dioxide and waste products her body produces. Once the umbilical cord is cut, your baby has her own closed circulatory system for the first time.

respiratory health In the womb, a baby's lungs are filled with fluid. During birth the fluid is squeezed out of the lungs by the contractions of the womb and the journey through the birth canal. At birth your baby breathes independently for the first time. Your baby's breathing may appear irregular at first, but settles into an effective rhythm within a few days. Babies have very small nasal passages that are prone to becoming blocked with mucus and other secretions. These passages expand as your baby gets older; her ability to breathe through her mouth will also improve.

digestive system Your baby's first food is milk because her digestive system is immature at birth. She will need to drink milk until this system has matured enough to cope with solid foods (after six months). In some cases, an infant's digestive tract may not be fully toned, which can lead to gas. An immature digestive system may be a contributory factor to colic (see page 12).

renal system A baby's renal system is vital for the efficient functioning of every other body system. Babies' kidneys, immature at birth, have to cope with the important functions of filtering blood and conserving water. Your baby's bladder is growing in size and she will not be able to control urination through her pelvic floor muscles. This ability begins to develop around two years of age, but varies from child to child.

key improvement areas

In the following ways, massage is a great way of maintaining and improving your baby's health:

bones

- Helps with good posture and balance
- Reduces muscle tension that could lead to more serious problems
- Increases nutrient flow to your baby's bones

breathing

- Improves breathing patterns
- Helps reduce any respiratory problems

digestion

- A good remedy for constipation
- Relieves gas
- Reduces water retention
- Cleans the blood by toning the kidneys

circulation

- Stimulates blood and lymph circulation
- Helps strengthen your baby's immune system
- Releases any toxins held in the body

muscles

- Relieves muscle tension and spasm
- Removes waste such as lactic acid that builds
  up after rigorous exercise
- Helps to build good muscle tone and increases
  joint flexibility
- Increases the flow of blood and nutrients
  to the muscles

nervous system

- Relaxes and calms your baby
- Helps your baby to sleep, if restlessness is a problem
- Raises endorphin levels, which promotes healing
  and a happy disposition
- Provides a safe and easy release from frustration
  and hyperactive behavior
- Generally balances your baby's energies

Emily had colic

Colic makes babies and their parents feel miserable. Babies who suffer from it often cry for more than three hours a day, three to four days a week! Although they may cry at any time, it usually worsens in the evening. A typical baby with colic will look very uncomfortable, or appear to be in pain. She may lift her head, draw her legs up to her stomach, become red in the face, and pass wind.

Naturally, all this discomfort can create stress and anxiety within the home. Parents and other family members often find it difficult to cope with the constant crying. The exact cause of colic isn't known—painful abdominal gas may contribute to it, but there's no direct evidence to prove that it's due to gastrointestinal problems. We *do* know that about 20 percent of all babies get colic, and that it appears at around two to four weeks of age and can last for three months, or longer in some cases.

Emily suffered from colic as a newborn baby. She often displayed signs of having pain in her stomach characterized by pulling her legs up to her chest, prolonged bouts of crying and being unsettled, and tension in the abdomen area. She also found it difficult to deal with wind after feeding, and regularly suffered from constipation. All this discomfort contributed to an irregular sleeping and feeding pattern that made it difficult for her to settle.

Emily's parents decided to massage her stomach area twice a day for two weeks using the strokes recommended for the stomach. Although Emily's colic did not improve immediately, by the end of the two week period, she was certainly suffering less from wind and constipation. She was also much more settled during the day. Her parents continued to massage her stomach once a day and found that her colic was greatly reduced.

27

2 getting started

the right environment for massage

It is important that both you and your baby feel relaxed and comfortable in your environment before you begin to massage. Before you start, think about what would make you feel most relaxed, both physically and mentally.

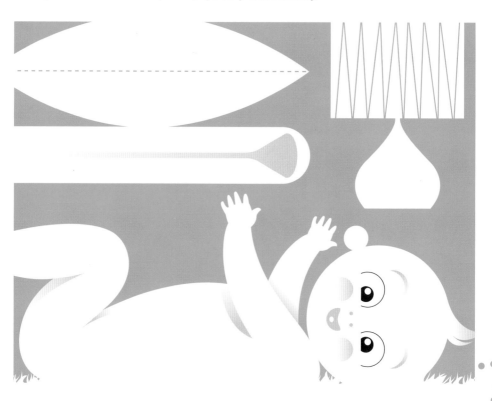

temperature

Make the room you choose for massage comfortably warm for your baby. You may want to remove all his clothes for the massage, so as you work, keep checking that he is not too cold or hot, as this might affect his enjoyment of the experience.

lighting

For much of the massage routine, your baby lies on his back. Switch off or dim overhead lights to prevent bright light from shining in his eyes. This might distract your baby and prevent good eye contact. Natural daylight or side lamps create a much more relaxing environment.

noise

If possible, choose a time for massage when noises in and around the home are minimal. Loud or strange noises could distract your baby and prevent him from fully relaxing. Why not play soothing music in the background to create a calm atmosphere for the massage? This can enhance the experience for both of you.

space

Try to find the perfect space for massage at home. Whether this is in the bedroom, bathroom, or nursery, what's most important is that you both have enough space to be positioned comfortably. You also need room for paraphernalia including oils and diaper-changing equipment. Make sure you have everything on hand before you begin, to avoid having to interrupt the massage.

Before you start to massage your baby, make certain that your environment is quiet, comfortable, and free from distractions.

positioning the baby

You can massage a baby from many different positions. Whichever you choose, make it comfortable for both of you and keep your back well supported with pillows or rolled towels as necessary.

raised positions

Massaging your baby sitting on a bed or standing beside a raised changing table can be comfortable and convenient, especially if the massage forms part of a bedtime routine. The disadvantage is the danger that your baby could fall and hurt himself.

floor positions

Massaging your baby on a mat on the floor has the advantage that there is usually plenty of space and no danger of the baby falling and hurting himself. Some people find sitting on the floor uncomfortable: experiment with some of the positions below, adapting them to suit you and your baby.

cradling Sit on your bottom with the soles of your feet touching so your legs make a diamond shape. Place your baby between your legs with his head resting gently on your shins/ankles. This position comfortably elevates your baby's head from the floor. Since it helps create a small, secure environment, this position is particularly good for massaging young babies.

It is important that both you and your baby are comfortable while you are massaging him.

legs straddled Sit on your bottom with legs outstretched on either side of your baby. Use a wall to support your back, if necessary.

kneeling Sit on a soft cushion or mat with legs crossed beneath you. Place your baby on a mat or blanket in front of you.

asking your baby's permission

Massage is a very intimate personal experience. It is important to show your baby
the same respect for his body and personal space as you would accord an adult.
Babies, too, have different needs and emotional states, and may not always wish to be
massaged. An unwanted massage could cause your baby to become unhappy or tense.

before you start

To make absolutely sure that your baby is ready for his massage you should always ask his permission to begin. This may sound strange: he can't verbally tell you he would like a massage, but he can subtly communicate whether he likes or dislikes something through body language and vocal sounds.

communicating during massage

Observing your baby's behavior during the routine enhances the experience and improves overall communication between you because it gives you the opportunity to learn more about your baby's signs and cues. Try to identify his cues before you massage and throughout the session to understand the ways in which he shows his preferences and objections for different strokes.

signs that a baby is relaxed and ready for massage Good eye contact, relaxed arms and legs, regular breathing pattern, cooing or other vocalizing.

signs that a baby may not want a massage Crying, jittery arm and leg movements, frowning, lack of eye contact.

Your baby might not always be in the mood for a massage. Remember to observe his behavior and gauge his enjoyment before you unsettle him with an unwanted massage.

what if my baby cries?

Crying during part of the massage is perfectly normal. It does not mean you are doing something wrong, or that your baby does not like massage. If you sense that your baby has had enough massage, stop and try again another day. Remember, you are learning about massage together.

massage and music

Your voice is comforting and soothing for your baby, so talking or singing to him during massage enhances the experience for him.

If your baby starts to cry while you are massaging him, do not assume that he is unhappy. He may simply need time to get used to this new sensation.

for foot massage
This little piggy went to market (roll big toe)
This little piggy stayed at home (roll second toe)
This little piggy had roast beef (roll third toe)
This little piggy had none (roll fourth toe)
And this little piggy...went fast to sleep, before we even noticed (roll little toe, then wrap fingers around baby's foot and hold for a few seconds)

for face and body massage
Cheek, chin (stroke from cheek to chin)
Cheek, chin (stroke from cheek to chin)
Cheek, chin (stroke from cheek to chin)
Nose! (stroke the nose)

Cheek, chin (stroke from cheek to chin)
Cheek, chin (stroke from cheek to chin)
Cheek, chin (stroke from cheek to chin)
Toes! (stroke the toes)

using oils

The best oils for baby massage are organic, first-pressed, vegetable-based products, such as grape seed or sunflower seed oil. Olive oil is excellent for babies with particularly dry skin. These oils are entirely natural, containing no artificial additives or preservatives. They're inexpensive, and readily available from your local health food store or supermarket. If you prefer a product specifically blended for baby massage, browse upscale beauty-care stores and natural babycare outlets, or search the internet. Always follow the manufacturer's instructions for use.

caution Babies may have allergies to peanuts and/or wheat. To minimize the risk of an allergic action, avoid oils that contain nut extracts, such as peanut oil or sweet almond oil, or wheat extracts, such as wheatgerm oil.

essential oils

Aromatherapists blend essential oils—the highly concentrated essence of the plant—in a carrier oil such as grape seed and apply them to the skin through massage to treat physical and emotional ailments. Essential oils have many therapeutic benefits, but they are chemical substances that can be dangerous if used incorrectly and without the advice of a qualified aromatherapist. Unless you have some knowledge of aromatherapy, you should not use essential oils for baby massage. To incorporate essential oils safely into your routine, heat a few drops in a room vaporizer. Essential oil of lavender can be particularly relaxing and helps to create a peaceful environment.

Essential oils are well known for their therapeutic benefits but you should only use them for baby massage if you have some knowledge of aromatherapy. Why not use olive oil instead, which is entirely natural, inexpensive, and excellent for babies with dry skin.

familiarizing your baby with touch

Massage should always be introduced slowly and at your baby's pace so that he feels comfortable with the movements. Two minutes of massage on a relaxed baby has much greater benefit than ten minutes of massage on an unhappy baby. Try some of the following techniques to help relax your baby and get him used to your touch.

touch through clothes

Some small babies do not like having their clothes removed. Gently stroking his back through his clothing may help a baby feel more comfortable about being touched and familiarize him with the pleasurable sensation of massage.

skin-to-skin contact

Spending time with your baby skin-to-skin can encourage him to feel more relaxed without clothes.

relaxed touch technique

This is a technique that teaches babies to relax. Try to make eye contact with your baby. Rest one hand gently on his leg near the thigh, your other hand on his shin; hold for a few moments. Gently bounce your baby's leg and tell him in a relaxing and soothing voice to relax until you feel his muscles begin to ease. When you feel your baby's leg relax, congratulate him on his achievement. Practiced regularly, this exercise helps your baby learn to recognize the sensation of relaxation so that he relaxes more easily.

firm touch

Infants generally enjoy confident touch and handling, but you should never touch your baby so firmly that you cause him discomfort. Keep your strokes confident but gentle. Through practice you'll discover the level of touch he prefers.

Your baby may not like having his clothes removed so try spending time with him, skin-to-skin, to accustom him to your touch.

when to massage

The best time to massage your baby is a time that suits you both. Generally the best time for infant massage is when your baby has rested and is neither too full nor too hungry. It's important that the massage is unhurried, so choose a time when there are unlikely to be other demands and you can focus on your baby. Build the massage into his daily routine and he will begin to anticipate the session and feel relaxed and comfortable when the strokes begin. Babies like repetition and feel secure knowing which activity follows which.

when not to massage

There are times when massage is not considered safe or comfortable for your baby. If he has any of the following health conditions, skip the massage:

- acute infections
- fever
- sickness
- diarrhea
- undiagnosed lumps and bumps
- contagious disease
- serious skin complaints
- open sores
- inflammation
- immunization in the past 72 hours
- recent surgery

There may be other times when you feel it would be inappropriate to massage your baby. Always listen to your instinct when deciding whether or not to massage.

Always make sure your baby is happy to be massaged. Choose a time of day when both of you are relaxed and make the massage part of the daily routine.

Christopher's new teeth

The emergence of a baby's first tooth is not always a peaceful event! Many parents notice that a previously calm infant becomes tetchy and irritable, doesn't appear to be feeding well, drools constantly, compulsively chews on anything at hand, and may also develop a diaper rash.

All these symptoms may be due to teething. The teething process causes various chemical changes in the gum tissue, which allow the teeth to grow through, and it is these chemical changes which may cause your baby discomfort, and result in any or all of the symptoms mentioned.

So when should a parent expect this to happen? The answer is, it varies. The first teeth, (also called milk teeth or baby teeth) usually appear around 6 months. But some babies get them earlier, others noticeably later— even up to a year!

Christopher suffered from teething pains from when he was five months old. Teething pains would wake him at night and affect his appetite. He was also unsettled in the day. His parents used the massage strokes for the face and particularly the gums and jaw frequently throughout the day when he appeared to be in discomfort. The massage helped him relax and seemed to help him cope with sore and irritated gums. The massage helped Christopher to cope with the discomfort of teething and provided his parents with a practical tool they could use when their son was in pain.

3   head-to-toe massage

starting the session

This massage routine is made up of a variety of strokes adapted from different therapeutic practices across the world. It includes massage strokes from India that are designed to relieve tension in the body, techniques from Sweden to aid and boost circulation, and pressure-point work based on the practice of reflexology that treats the body's ailments through the stimulation of specific areas of the foot.

Most babies seem to enjoy having their legs stroked, so begin the massage there. Feet are also a good place to touch—you will probably get lots of giggles and smiles!

relaxed parent, relaxed baby

Before you start to massage your baby, it is important to relax yourself: even tiny babies are sensitive to their parents' moods. Take time at the beginning of the massage to ease out tension in your mind and body so the routine becomes a positive experience for both of you. First relax your shoulders by rolling them forward and backward a number of times; think about stretching your arms in the air. Take some deep breaths and visualize a peaceful and tranquil scene to boost your sense of inner calm.

massaging the legs and feet

Most babies enjoy having their legs stroked, so this makes a good place to start a massage routine. Babies seem to feel relaxed having their legs massaged because the area is touched regularly during diaper changing and washing. Babies' feet and toes are very sensitive, and foot massage usually elicits happy smiles from your baby! By starting with a nonintrusive, nonthreatening area of the body, you will begin to gain your baby's confidence.

to begin Find a position that is comfortable for you and your baby. Take off your baby's clothes. Remove her diaper if you are happy to do so. Lay your baby on her back with her feet closest to your body.

ask permission Remember to ask your baby's permission to massage before you begin so that she has the opportunity to let you know whether now is a good time. Make eye contact and ask your baby, "Are you ready for your massage?" If she seems relaxed and content, you may begin.

leg massage

Because infants can hold tension in their legs, start by relaxing the whole area: rest one hand gently on your baby's leg near the thigh, the other hand on her shin. Hold the position for a few moments. Gently bounce your baby's leg and tell her to relax in a soothing voice until you feel her leg begin to ease. When you sense this relaxation, congratulate your baby on her achievement.
Repeat on the other leg.

massage tips
- introduce strokes slowly and gently, working at your baby's pace.
- keep the strokes long, flowing, and rhythmical. This makes the massage more relaxing for your baby and helps you establish a good rhythm.
- observe your baby during the massage. Keep checking that she is enjoying the strokes. Give her time to settle and become familiar with them.
- never force your baby to continue a massage if she becomes unhappy or tense.

Indian draining

This stroke comes from Indian massage. Raise your baby's leg and secure the ankle with one hand. Place your other hand at the base of her thigh. Gently glide your lower hand up the length of the leg until you reach the ankle. Swap hands so the hand that has just been massaging secures the ankle and the other hand rests at the base of the thigh. Repeat the gliding motion up to the ankle. Change hands again. Repeat the stroke six to eight times.

Try this gentle form of Indian draining six to eight times on each leg to encourage the circulation in your baby's feet.

- relieves muscular tension in the legs (your baby spends a great deal of time kicking her legs in the air!)
- helps warm your baby's feet by encouraging circulation.

leg wringing

Place your hands beside each other at the base of the thigh. Gently wrap your fingers around the thigh. Move your hands up the length of the thigh in a gliding motion as if wringing something out. Do not squeeze the thigh; simply glide. When you reach the ankle, replace your hands at the starting position ready to begin again. Repeat six to eight times.

- helps relieve muscular tension by massaging across the muscle.
- encourages relaxation of the leg muscles.

Swedish draining

This stroke originates in Swedish massage techniques. It is similar to Indian draining except your hands move toward the body. Raise your baby's leg and secure the ankle with one hand. Place your other hand at the base of her thigh. Gently glide your lower hand down the length of the leg to the ankle. Swap hands so that the hand that has been massaging secures the ankle. Repeat the gliding motion down to the base of the thigh. Change hands again. You should repeat the stroke six to eight times.

- boosts circulation by supporting the blood's journey back to the heart. The optimum circulation of the blood is immensely important for your baby's health and wellbeing. When her body has good circulation, every cell in her body receives an excellent supply of oxygen and nutrients from her blood—and these are vital for growth and tissue repair.

Gliding your hand up and down your baby's leg improves the circulation and relieves muscular tension.

rolling

Elevate your baby's leg. Place both your hands on either side of the base of her thigh. Open your hands and gently roll the leg between them. Roll from thigh to ankle. Repeat three times. Try singing "Rolling, Rolling, Rolling" as you perform the stroke. Your baby will love this!

• helps relax all the muscles of the leg.

foot massage

sole stroking Cradle your baby's foot in your hands, sole facing you, and gently stroke from heel to toes. Repeat six to eight times.

toe rolling Take each toe in turn and roll it. Try singing a rhyme, such as "This Little Piggy" while massaging the toes.

pressure points

Hold the baby's foot in your hand. Extend your first finger and place it under the ball of the foot. Hold the position for a few seconds. Now move your finger to the arch of the foot. As before, press gently into the arch for a few seconds. Repeat three times.

- according to the practice of reflexology, the area of the foot under the toes relates to your baby's sinuses and head. By stimulating this area, you can help treat sinus problems.
- in reflexology, the arch of the foot corresponds to your baby's diaphragm and digestive system. Massage this pressure point if your baby suffers from colic.

Concentrating your massage techniques on your baby's feet not only employs the age-old benefits of reflexology, but also elicits squeals of delight from your baby!

walking thumbs

Cradling your baby's foot, gently pad and press all around the sole with the flat part of your thumb.

relaxed foot

Turn the foot over to expose the top of the foot. Using the flat part of your thumb, stroke from toes to ankle using a rhythmical motion. Repeat six times.

ankle circles

Place your fingers at the ankle joint. Make small circles around it. This encourages a good flow of blood to the joint, helping keep it supple. It also eases tired muscles in the area. Now repeat all the strokes from pages 50–56 on the other leg and foot.

finishing the legs

buttock circles Place your hands under your baby's buttocks. Using your fingers, make little circles on the buttocks. Repeat six to eight times.

leg stretches Gently encourage your baby to stretch out her legs by stroking from the top of the thighs to the ankles. Repeat six times.

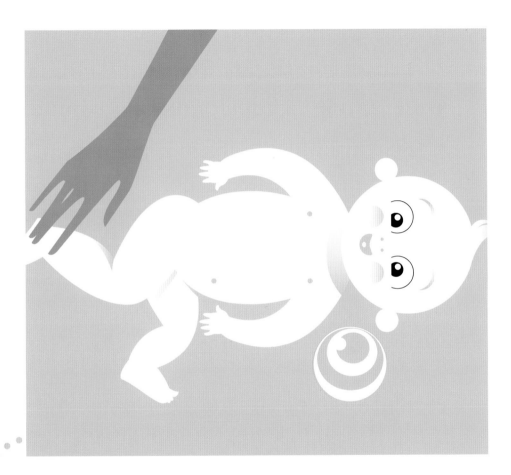

Ankle circles are particularly good for babies when they are learning to crawl or walk—the ankle joint is put under great stress during these periods.

Placing your hand on your baby's tummy is as soothing for her as a hot-water bottle. Just remember that massaging the stomach can displace trapped air in your baby's tummy, causing some discomfort. Simply observe your baby's reactions and be gentle.

massaging the stomach

The abdomen can be a sensitive area to massage because strokes here can aid the passage of trapped air bubbles in your baby's tummy and intestines and move them toward the bowel. Stomach massage can have huge benefits for babies who suffer excessive or trapped gas or bouts of constipation. Some babies find the sensation of air moving around the stomach uncomfortable, however, and can become tense. If this happens, you must decide whether to continue the massage. Releasing the trapped air will help relieve your baby of the pain of trapped gas, which may outweigh the minor discomfort she feels as the air moves around her stomach. As she becomes more familiar with stomach massage, she will become less sensitive to the strokes.

resting hand

Make contact with your baby's tummy by laying your hand flat across the soft part of the stomach. Rest it here for 30 seconds or more.

• gets your baby used to the feel of your hands on her stomach.
• heat from your hand acts like a mini hot-water bottle–very soothing and reassuring if your baby has a tummy ache.

stomach paddling

Place your hand flat across the soft part of your baby's tummy. Move your hand from the top of the stomach area to the bottom of the stomach area. Repeat the movement with your other hand. Repeat six to eight times, using alternate hands in a paddling motion. Be sure to use the flat part of your hand, not the edge.

elevated stomach paddling

Hold your baby's legs by the ankles with one hand. Elevate the legs and with the other hand, repeat the paddling motion described on the preceding page. Repeat six to eight times.

side strokes

Place the pad of each thumb on either side of your baby's tummy button. Gently apply a little pressure to the tummy as you glide your thumbs to the outside of the stomach area. Use gentle but firm pressure, being careful not to press too hard. Repeat six to eight times.

full circle

Using the fingers of one hand, make circles in a clockwise direction over your baby's stomach area. This follows the direction of digestion. Do not press too hard. Repeat six to eight times.

upside-down "U"

Using the fingers of one hand, draw an upside-down "U" or bridge from the right side of your baby's stomach to the left. Repeat six to eight times.

walking fingers

Open your hand and gently drum your fingers from the bottom of your baby's stomach to the top as you walk your fingers from the right side of your baby's tummy across to the left. Repeat six to eight times. Make the strokes gradually lighter to signal that the stomach massage is coming to an end.

• helps break down large air bubbles trapped in the stomach. The smaller these are, the easier and less painful they are to pass.

Making a full circle in a clockwise direction over your baby's stomach aids her digestion by breaking down any trapped air bubbles.

The chest area can be sensitive for your baby, so give her time to get used to the idea of being massaged there by simply resting your hands on her chest first.

massaging the chest

The chest is a very vulnerable area for your baby because it houses the heart and lungs. When you massage her chest, she may tense her arms and cover her chest as she instinctively tries to protect this sensitive area. If this happens, try to relax her by getting her used to the feel of your hands—rest them without moving on her chest area. This helps soothe tension and reassures your baby. She will soon start to relax.

draw a heart

Place your hands upright on either side of your baby's chest, palms down. Gently and slowly move your hands toward your baby's shoulders and neck, drawing the shape of a heart. Come back to your starting position and repeat six to eight times.

draw a cross

Place your hands upright on either side of your baby's chest as before. Gently move one hand diagonally across the chest to the shoulder, then back to its starting position. Gently move the other hand diagonally across the chest to the opposite shoulder and back to its starting point, drawing an "X"-shaped cross over your baby's chest. Repeat six to eight times.

- both strokes help increase your baby's lung capacity by relaxing the muscles of her chest and the accessory breathing muscles.
- loosens mucus in the chest area; this is a particularly effective stroke when your baby has a cold or chest infection.

massaging the arms and hands

When working on the arms and the hands, it is important to recognize that many babies enjoy sucking their fingers or thumb for comfort. Massage sometimes interrupts this, which might make her tense. If your baby enjoys sucking her thumb or fingers, you may find that you need to thoroughly relax her arm and hand before starting the massage.

arm massage

Start by relaxing the arm: rest your hands gently on your baby's upper and lower arm for a few moments. Gently bounce the arm, telling her in a soothing voice to relax until you feel the limb begin to ease. When you feel your baby relax, congratulate her on her achievement.

pit stroking Gently elevate your baby's arm and, using your first and second fingers, stroke the inside of the arm from the elbow, into the armpit and down the side of the chest. Make your strokes quite firm. Repeat six times.

If you think your baby might be coming down with a cold, stroke the inside of her arm. This helps boost the immune system.

• stimulates the lymphatic system by encouraging the flow of lymph from the arm into the lymph nodes in the armpit. Aiding lymphatic drainage helps boost your baby's immune system and encourages the removal of toxins from the body. This is a great stroke when you suspect your baby might be coming down with a cold: it helps your baby's immune system fight it off.

Indian draining

This is similar to the Indian draining you performed on the leg. Raise your baby's arm and secure the wrist with one hand. Place your other hand around the top of the arm, next to the shoulder. Gently glide your lower hand up the length of the arm to the wrist. Swap hands, securing the wrist with the hand that has just been massaging, and placing the other hand around the top of the shoulder. Repeat the gliding motion up to the wrist. Change hands again. Repeat six to eight times.

• helps relieve muscular tension in the arm.
• boosts circulation to the hand: because of their developing circulatory system, many babies suffer from cold hands.

arm wringing

In a wringing technique, tissues are compressed against one another and gently "wrung" as your hands move alternately across the long axis of the muscle, and stretch the tissue. The stroke resembles the wringing you practiced on your baby's leg.

Place your hands around the top of your baby's arm at the shoulder, one beside the other. Gently wrap your fingers around the upper arm. Move your hands up the length of the arm in a gliding motion, as if wringing something out. Do not squeeze, simply glide. When you reach the wrist replace your hands at the top of the upper arm, ready to repeat the stroke. Repeat six to eight times.

• relieves muscular tension by massaging across the muscles of the arm.

hand massage

finger rolling Hold your baby's hand and gently roll the thumb and each finger in a clockwise direction.

• encourages the development of your baby's grasp.

wrist circles

With your thumb and first finger, gently make little circles around your baby's wrist.

• helps encourage good blood flow to the wrist joint to keep it supple and healthy. Like the ankle joint, the wrist suffers heavy impact when your baby starts to crawl. Massage helps to soothe any stiffness.

Swedish draining

Elevate your baby's arm and secure the wrist with one hand. Place your other hand at the wrist, then gently glide it down the length of the arm to the top of the upper arm at the shoulder joint. Swap hands so the hand that has been massaging secures the wrist and glide your other hand down the length of the arm to the top of the upper arm again. Repeat the stroke using alternate hands six to eight times.

rolling

To help relax your baby's arm, place both hands on either side of the upper arm near the shoulder joint. Gently roll your hands along the arm until you reach the wrist. Place your hands at the top of the upper arm and repeat again. Try singing "Rolling, Rolling, Rolling." Repeat the stroke six to eight times. Repeat all the strokes from pages 65–67 on the other arm and hand.

massaging the face

Massaging the face can be very relaxing and also has excellent therapeutic benefits, particularly for teething babies and those with congested sinuses. When massaging the face, apply only the tiniest amount of oil to your fingertips to prevent it from entering the baby's eyes, nose, or mouth. For peace of mind, choose 100 percent organic vegetable-derived oils (see page 38).

When you massage your baby's face, you may find that she starts to root for milk to suckle: this is because the sensation of fingertips on her cheek can resemble a nipple. This might make her irritable. Stop the massage for a feeding, if necessary, and start again later. Most babies enjoy the relaxing sensation of facial massage—if you have had a facial you will know how enjoyable the experience can be. However, some find facial massage overwhelming. Your fingers are very large in comparison to your baby's face, and some infants become tense when fingers cover their eyes, breaking eye contact. If so, pick one or two strokes that are comfortable for your baby and practice these until she is more confident with the facial routine. You may find your baby moves her face during the massage as she tries to investigate your fingers!

open brow

Make a triangle shape on your baby's forehead with your thumbs, being careful not to cover her eyes. Gently glide each thumb across the brow to your baby's temples. Do not put any pressure on the temple area. Repeat the gliding motion six to eight times.

stroke over eyebrows

Gently place your first fingers on your baby's eyebrows, close to the bridge of the nose. Gently stroke across the eyebrows. Repeat six to eight times.

Massaging your baby's face is an excellent way of relieving any pain she might have from teething and congested sinuses.

clear nose

Place your first fingers on either side of your baby's nose, at the base of the nostrils. Gently glide your fingers up to the bridge of the nose until you reach your baby's tear ducts. Bring your fingers back down the nose until you reach the cheekbones. Follow the shape of your baby's cheekbones across her face until you reach the ears. Now stroke your fingers up and over the ears, under the chin, and toward the throat.

• helps move mucus out of the congested passages toward the lymphatic system. Newborns have very compressed, narrow nasal passages which make clearing the nose difficult when they have sinus congestion. Sinus congestion often results in poor sleeping and feeding.

happy smiles

Baby has a blocked nose? Try this simple technique—it brings her rapid relief.

The following stroke is a wonderfully effective technique for relieving the teething pains that often make babies miserable. Teething can start when a baby is as young as three months of age. Place your first fingers along her top lip, pointing toward each other. Gently move each finger in opposite directions along the top lip following the line of the gums. Repeat the stroke on the bottom lip, again tracing the shape of your baby's gums.

• helps relieve teething pain by putting pressure on a baby's sore gums through the lips. You need to press fairly firmly to relieve pain: think of a time when you may have hurt yourself and squeezing or putting pressure on the area helped to ease the discomfort.

cheek circles

This is another excellent stroke for relaxing your baby's jaw when she is experiencing teething discomfort. Place the first and second fingers of each hand on either side of your baby's cheeks where there is a small dip. Gently make small circles with your fingers in either direction. Repeat for thirty seconds.

massaging the back

Back massage is great for your baby not only because it helps to relax and strengthen the muscles of the back, but also because it gives your infant a short spell lying on her tummy. Today, babies don't tend to spend much time on their stomachs because of the guidelines that recommend that they sleep on their backs. Encouraging your baby to spend some minutes on her tummy everyday, under your supervision, helps strengthen the back, neck, and upper body muscles. It may also help your baby to crawl, an important stage in her development. Lying on her tummy offers your baby a different view of the world, allowing her to discover new sensations and have a novel experience of her environment.

beginning the massage

Place your baby on the floor horizontally in front of you. To make this position comfortable for her, position her arms out in front. It is easier to massage your baby's back without her diaper on, so you may wish to lie your baby on some extra towels in case she pees or poops. If your baby is very small or does not like to lie on her front, place her horizontally across your knees rather than directly on the floor. This should help her feel less claustrophobic and offer the security of your body.

back paddling

Place your hands beside each other, palms down, at the top of your baby's back. Gently move your hands back and forth, working down the baby's back toward her bottom. When you get to her buttocks, replace your hands in the starting position and repeat six to eight times.

Lying your baby on her tummy to massage her back allows her a whole new perspective on the world! It also helps strengthen the back, neck, and upper body muscles.

back stroking

Cup one hand around your baby's buttocks. Place the other hand at the top of your baby's back and gently stroke down to the buttocks. Repeat the stroke six to eight times.

small circles

Place the first and second fingers of both hands at the top of your baby's back on either side of the spine. Make small circles with your fingers, moving down the back until you reach the buttocks. Here, make bigger circles to relax the muscles. Return to the top of the baby's back and repeat the stroke six to eight times.

combing

Open the fingers of one hand and place it, palm down, on your baby's back. Position your hand so your baby's spine sits between your fingers. Gently comb down the back to the buttocks, keeping the spine in the gap between the fingers so that you do not place any pressure on it. Repeat the stroke six to eight times. As the massage comes to an end, make the strokes lighter and lighter to indicate to your baby that the massage is finishing. This aids communication between you.

Try to massage the muscles on either side of the spine. Be careful not to press on your baby's spine itself, which is delicate and bony.

Jenny wouldn't sleep

case history

3

Some babies seem to be on the go all the time. And that means they not only find it hard to get to sleep, they don't seem to stay asleep for very long either! Parents of babies who don't sleep very much often notice that they are highly reactive; consequently, any extra excitement such as a party, play session, or even a visit to grandma can have them going into overdrive very quickly. It seems that not only are they more sensitive to stimulation than other babies, but extra new sights and sounds can overwhelm them too.

As for sessions of boisterous play close to bedtime—this can lead to a troubled night ahead. It's a cocktail of excitement, tiredness, and tension that combine to keep your infant from settling down at the end of the day.

Jenny was a highly spirited baby who was difficult to settle to sleep. She slept infrequently in the day, which resulted in her becoming overtired by the evening. She often cried herself to sleep due to overstimulation and frustration. Jenny's parents decided to use massage to help her calm down toward the end of the day and to help her relax.

They started to massage Jenny's legs after her bath in the evening before bedtime. At first Jenny did not respond well to the massage, as it added to her overtiredness with yet another form of stimulation. Her parents then decided to try to massage her in the late afternoon before she became too tired, instead of playing with her and her toys. By introducing a relaxing afternoon activity as opposed to a stimulating one using play, they found that Jenny began to be more relaxed around bedtime, and as a result became easier to settle in the evening. Eventually her sleeping pattern became more regular, and she went to bed without tears.

4 massage & movement

gentle stretches

After you have massaged your baby, you may like to incorporate some gentle stretches into your routine. Gently moving and stretching your baby's arms and legs encourages flexibility in his hip and shoulder joints, gives your baby gentle exercise, and allows you to have fun and make him smile!

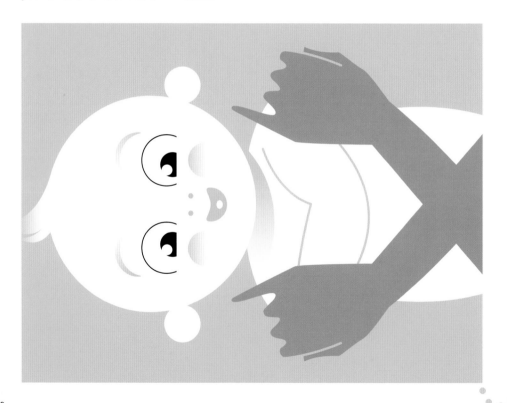

bear hug

Place your baby on the floor, lying vertically in front of you. Gently hold your baby by his forearms and bring his arms to the center of his chest, crossing them in the middle. Your baby gives himself a hug with his arms! Gently hold the arms together in this position for a few seconds, then release. Repeat the movement, changing the arm at the front of the "hug." Repeat this movement six times, alternating the arm in front.

hand to toe

Hold your baby's right forearm with your right hand and his left calf with your left hand. Gently bring your baby's right arm and left leg to the center of his body, crossing leg over arm. Take the arm and leg back to the starting position and relax the limbs. Repeat with your baby's left forearm and right calf. Repeat the whole movement six times.

Gentle stretching is beneficial to your baby but seek medical advice first if he has ever suffered from problems with his joints.

legs up and down

Hold baby's legs with both hands around the shin and calf. Gently encourage him to bend his legs and bring them toward his chest and tummy. Hold in position for five seconds, then release. Repeat six times.

• releases trapped gas by gently compressing the intestines and encouraging trapped air to be expelled from the body. Try it if your baby has colic or suffers from painful gas.

massage and settling techniques

There are a number of settling techniques you can combine with massage to help calm and soothe your baby. You may find the techniques particularly useful if you have a baby who suffers from overstimulation or finds it difficult to settle and relax. These techniques can be practiced before a massage to help relax your baby or performed whenever he is feeling tense. You don't need to remove your baby's clothes before practicing these methods.

Indian bouncing

Indian mothers use this technique to soothe their babies. Sit on the floor with your legs stretched out in front of you. Alternatively, sit on a chair or sofa. Place your baby across your lap, face down. Make sure your baby's head and neck are well supported by your legs. Gently move your knees up and down in a rhythmical motion so that your baby gently bobs up and down on your lap. While moving your knees calmly, pat the baby on the back with flat palms, synchronizing the rhythm with your knee movements.

baby swaying

This position provides your baby with a new view of his environment and the slight pressure on his abdomen helps release trapped gas. Make a cradle with your arms and place your baby inside it, face down, with his arms and legs hanging on either side of your arms. Place your hand on his tummy. Make sure his head is well supported in the crook of your elbow. Gently sway your baby from side to side.

Applying slight pressure to the stomach helps ease trapped gas. Rhythmical movements are also very soothing, and patting replicates the sound of a mother's heartbeat.

caution: Make sure you have a good hold on your baby before you begin to sway.

adapting the massage
to your growing child

As your baby grows, he will naturally begin to want to investigate his environment and everything around him. Babies are thirsty for knowledge and curious about almost everything. When your baby becomes more mobile, you will find it difficult to stop him from venturing off to discover new things, and he may not want to stay in one place for a massage. You might be concerned that this desire to move around would pose a problem for massage. Don't worry! All that is required is some adaptation of the original routine, a little flexibility, and lots of patience!

the curious baby

Once your baby is crawling, he might not be as interested as he once was in receiving a massage. His prime concern now is exploring his environment. However, your baby still needs massage, even if he might not want to stay in one place to receive it. Indeed, massage during this period is especially important because your baby is using and developing his muscles every day through physical exertion. Instead of performing the full routine, try practicing sections as the opportunity arises. While your baby is sitting up playing with a toy, massage his back, hands, or feet. Massage his legs after diaper-changing and stroke his forehead while he is having a bottle or nursing.

It is always important to respect your baby's wishes. If exploring is more important than massage, don't force your baby to stay still. If you do, the result will be an unhappy baby and a tense parent.

the toddler years (ages 1–3)

This is a time during which your baby grows in confidence and becomes more independent. You may find that your toddler often becomes frustrated as he struggles to learn about sharing, thinking of others, and following directions and routines. The toddler years are also marked by an increase in tantrums as your child's self-awareness grows.

fitting in massage time

Toddlers love to learn and investigate new things. Massage offers your toddler the opportunity to experience new sensations, not to mention making a mess with lots of oil! Not all toddlers want to be massaged, however; the toddler years are a time when your child learns he has the choice of saying "no" to certain activities. Many toddlers also have a very short attention span and become tense if asked to stay in one place for too long. You may still be able to practice nonintrusive massage with your toddler when he is feeling settled, but it's essential to follow his cue or you may both become tense.

massage fun and games

Make massage fun for your toddler by combining it with songs, action, and counting games such as "This Little Piggy." You can make up your own massage routine to include your child's favorite nursery rhymes and strokes that you know he enjoys. The key to helping toddlers stay happy with massage is to keep it enjoyable!

Why not combine massage time with your toddler's favorite nursery rhymes? Toddlers tend to have a short attention span, so making the massage fun will keep him amused for longer.

preschool fun

When children reach the age of three or four, their attention span starts to lengthen and they may become interested in playing games with you and other siblings rather than playing on their own. This is a great time to capture their imagination with massage. Massage is very beneficial for the preschool child, helping physiological complaints such as growing pains and muscular aches, and encouraging communication and closeness between parent and child.

massage for teddy

Some children immediately enjoy massage and may even offer to give their parents, siblings, or dollies/teddies a massage. Other fun ways to interest this age group in massage include games such as tracing the shape of letters on your child's back and asking him to guess them. Work with numbers and words, too, to make learning fun. These massage games are easy to play without removing clothes.

enticing the child

To introduce massage to a preschool child for the first time, you might like to link it to your child's hobby—why not suggest they have a "soccer player's massage" or a "ballerina's massage?" This makes the strokes seem extra special.

If your child really takes an interest in massage, he may even get his teddies or toys involved! If he is less enthusiastic about it, try to incorporate games into the massage.

the growing child

There are now calls for massage to be introduced into schools, with pupils learning how to practice clothed massage games on each other in the hope that they become more tactile and less aggressive toward each other. Swedish schools have promoted massage for a number of years, and studies show it helps reduce the rate of bullying between pupils and encourages more considerate behavior.

the future for massage

Once incorporated into your family life, massage becomes a communication tool that transcends childhood, bringing benefits in happiness and wellbeing that cannot be underestimated.
I hope practicing the routines in this book helps every member of your family experience these numerous blessings.

Massage is becoming such a popular form of relaxation and communication that it is being introduced into schools to promote calm behavior.

Tommy was tense

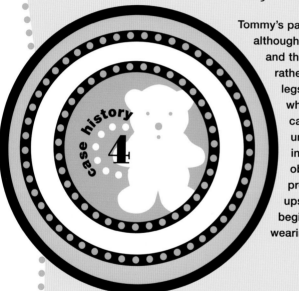

case history

4

Tommy's parents were aware that, although he was perfectly healthy and thriving, he was sometimes a rather tense baby. His arms and legs often went stiff and rigid when he was picked up and carried, and dressing and undressing him usually ended in tears because Tommy obviously found the whole process stressful and upsetting. His parents were beginning to find it equally wearing themselves.

Some babies do tense their arms and legs, and are unwilling to stretch out particularly when being bathed or being dressed. There's a logical explanation for this. Babies have a built-in instinct to survive which makes them very determined and strong despite their size. When you stretch out a baby's arms you expose the vital organs housed in the chest area—namely, the lungs and the heart. The baby's instinct is to cover and shield these areas from harm, attack, or threat. Stretching out a baby's arms can make him feel vulnerable. The curled fetal position of arms and legs tucked close to the body is a secure and reassuring position for a baby to be in, as it protected him so well in the womb.

Tommy's parents wanted to help him relax more. Gentle touch relaxation on the arms and legs together with gentle yoga stretches encouraged him to feel more at ease and comfortable. When Tommy became used to his parents touching his arms and legs, they also introduced some gentle massage strokes that were also designed to encourage him to relax and unwind. After a few weeks Tommy was much more relaxed, and dressing and bath time became easier and much more fun for everyone.

index

allergies 38

ankle circles 56, 57

arm massage 64–7

baby swaying 82

baby's development 12, 15, 21, 22–3, 24–5, 66

baby's wishes 34, 35, 49, 85

back massage 72–5

bear hug 81

body massage 37

bonding 6, 15, 16–17

buttock circles 56

cheek circles 71

chest massage 62–3

circulation 21, 22, 25, 51, 52, 66

clear nose 70–1

colds 63, 65

colic 12, 16, 26–7, 55, 81

combing 75

comfort 6, 12

communications 6, 16, 35

constipation 16, 24, 27, 59

contentedness 19, 25

cradle cap 13

crawling 85

crying 36

curiosity 85

digestive system 12, 23, 24, 55

draw a cross 63

draw a heart 63

eczema 13

elevated stomach paddling 60

essential oils 38

eye contact 15, 16, 17, 49, 68

face massage 37, 68–71

finger rolling 66

foot massage 37, 49, 55–7

full circle 60

fun and games 86–9

gas 12, 24, 59, 60, 81, 83

gentle stretches 80–1

hand massage 64, 66–7

hand to toe 81

handcare 19

happiness 19, 25

happy smiles 71

hormones 17, 18

Indian bouncing 82

Indian draining 51, 65–6

leg massage 49, 50–4

leg stretches 57

legs up and down 81

Ling, Henrik 11

love 6

marasmus 15

massage 6, 11, 48, 85
    baby's development

22–3, 24–5, 66
contraindications 43
older children 89–90
positioning the baby 32–3
preparation 19, 30–1,
34–5
timing 42
medical advice 4
muscles 21, 22, 24, 25
music 31, 37

nervous system 21, 25

oils 31, 38–9
open brow 68

paddling 59, 72
parental well-being 16, 26,
27, 49
pit stroking 65
postnatal depression 16
premature babies 11
pressure points 48, 55

reflexology 48, 55
relaxation 6, 16, 19, 41, 49,
63, 82, 92–3
relaxed foot 56
renal system 23, 24
respiratory health 23, 24,
63
resting hand 59
rolling 54, 67

safety considerations 4, 38,
51, 81, 83
school 90
settling techniques 82–3
side strokes 60
singing 15, 16, 17, 37
sinus 55, 68, 71
skeleton 22, 24
skin 13, 15, 21, 41
sleep problems 25, 76–7
small circles 75
smell 15, 16, 17
sole stroking 55
stimuli 15, 21

stomach massage 58–61
stress 16, 18, 27
stroke over eyebrows 69
stroking 75
Swedish draining 52, 67

talking 15, 16, 17, 37
teething 16, 44–5, 68, 71
tension 16, 19, 49, 50, 63,
82, 92–3
thumb sucking 64
toddlers 86–9
toe rolling 37, 55
touch 6, 12, 15, 16, 40–1

upside down "U" 60

vocalizing 15, 16, 17, 37

walking fingers 60
walking thumbs 56
wind 12, 26, 27
wringing 52, 66
wrist circles 67

dedication

To all my children for the experience of baby massage

Published by MQ Publications Limited
12 The Ivories, 6–8 Northampton Street
London N1 2HY
Tel: +44 (0) 20 7359 2244
Fax: +44 (0) 20 7359 1616
email: mail@mqpublications.com
website: www.mqpublications.com

Copyright © MQ Publications Limited 2005
Text © 2005 Gayle Berry
Illustrations © 2005 Bo Lundberg
Design: Lindsey Johns

ISBN: 1-84072-802-7
1 2 3 4 5 6 7 8 9

Printed and bound in China